BLACK HOLES

A TRUE BOOK

by
Paul P. Sipiera

Children's Press®
A Division of Grolier Publishing

New York London Hong Kong Sydney
Danbury, Connecticut

A rocky planet orbiting around a pulsar

Reading Consultant
Linda Cornwell
Learning Resource Consultant
Indiana Department of
Education

Science Consultant
Samuel Storch
Lecturer,
American Museum-Hayden
Planetarium, New York City

Dedication: To all my coworkers at William Rainey Harper College, my home for more than twenty years

Library of Congress Cataloging-in-Publication Data

Sipiera, Paul P.
    Black Holes / by Paul Sipiera.
        p.   cm. — (A true book)
    Includes bibliographical references and index.
    Summary: Explains the nature and formation of the cosmic phenomenon known as a black hole.
    ISBN 0-516-20326-6 (lib.bdg.)   0-516-26162-2 (pbk.)
    1.Black Holes (Astronomy)—Juvenile literature. [1. Black holes (Astronomy). I. Title. II. Series.
QB843.B55.S57 1997
523.8′ 875—dc20   96-36149
                                                        CIP
                                                        AC

Contents

A supernova (bright spot at bottom right) is an explosion that marks the end of the life of a massive star.

An Amazing Universe

Our universe contains many amazing things. Some stars are so massive that they have short lives before dying in violent explosions. Other stars contain so little mass that they seem to shine forever. Certain galaxies are seen to have giant explosions, while others simply collide. Although many planets orbit stars, most are not like the Earth. Our universe is filled with many unusual and wondrous things.

Perhaps the most mysterious of all cosmic things is a black hole. Most black holes form after a supernova—the explosion of a giant star. During such an explosion, a huge amount of matter is thrown into space. What is

An artist's impression of a supernova as seen from a nearby planetary system

left becomes crushed by gravity into a smaller and smaller object. The remains of the star, now called a "black hole," will seem to disappear from our universe.

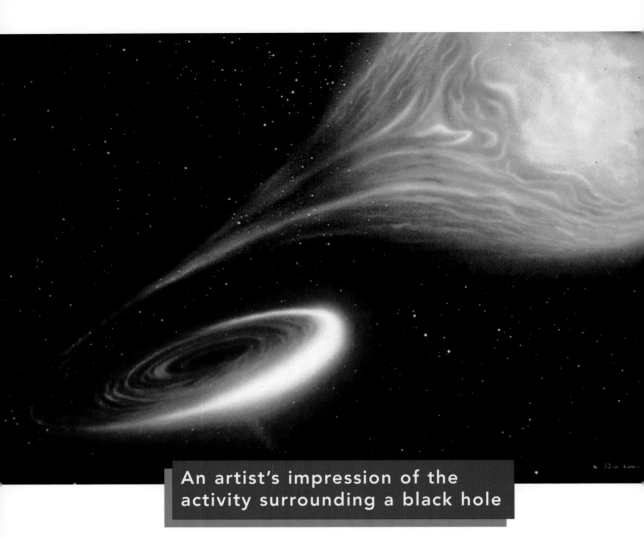

An artist's impression of the activity surrounding a black hole

It cannot be seen, because its gravity is so strong that it "pulls" all light into it.

Mass and Gravity

In order to understand a black hole, we must know something about mass and gravity. Mass is the quantity of material that makes up all things. Every object has mass. The mass of an object causes the object to attract other objects. This attraction is

If you let go of an object, the force of Earth's gravity will cause the object to fall downward.

called gravity. Put another way, gravity is the force of attraction between two masses.

Sometimes people confuse mass and weight. Weight is a measure of the force of gravity between an object and the Earth. When you weigh yourself on a scale, what the scale is really telling you is how hard the Earth's gravity is pulling on you. Astronauts in space do not feel this force because they are too far from

When in space, astronauts are weightless because they are far from the Earth and its pull is not as strong.

Earth. They are said to be "weightless," but they still have the same amount of mass as they have always had.

The amount of speed needed to escape the gravity of an object is called an escape velocity. If a rocket moves fast enough to escape Earth's gravity, it has reached its escape velocity. A rocket moving in a low orbit around Earth may be moving at 17,500 miles (28,000 kilometers) per hour.

A rocket needs to achieve great speed to escape the Earth's gravity.

To escape Earth's gravity and go to the Moon, the rocket must move faster than 25,000 miles (40,000 km) per hour, which is the escape velocity from Earth.

Because objects like Jupiter and the Sun are more massive than Earth, they have higher escape velocities. The more massive an object is, the stronger its gravity becomes.

To understand escape velocity, throw a ball straight up into the air. It will leave your hand quite fast, but it will go only so high. This is the force of gravity at work. It pulls your ball back down. If you throw the ball harder, it will go higher. But it will always fall back to the Earth. No baseball player could ever throw a ball fast enough to escape Earth's gravity.

On Deimos You'd Have Quite an Arm!

On Deimos, a tiny moon of Mars, the force of gravity is so low that almost anybody could toss a baseball into orbit around it.

The first person to use mathematics to describe gravity was Isaac Newton. He discovered that there is a force that moves the Moon around the Earth. He realized that this force explained the motion of not only the Earth

English physicist Isaac Newton (1642-1727) (right) discovered that gravity was the force that kept the moon in orbit around the Earth.

and Moon, but every object in the universe.

Newton also realized that the force of gravity grows weaker as two objects get farther apart. The opposite is also true. The closer two objects are, the stronger gravity becomes. In this way, Newton's discovery predicted a black hole. If an object can be made very small without losing any mass, it will then have the strongest possible gravity.

A Black Hole

Newton's discovery of gravity provided scientists with the idea of a black hole. In the early 1900s, the work of physicist Albert Einstein made the concept of a black hole even more possible. In studying Einstein's general theory of relativity,

This drawing (above) is an artist's impression of a black hole pulling in material from a companion star. The theories of German-born American physicist Albert Einstein (left) gave support to the idea that black holes exist.

astronomer Karl Schwartzchild realized that any object could become a black hole. All it has to do is to become small enough and dense enough.

If the Earth could be squeezed into a ball a half inch (1.2 centimeters) across, it would become a black hole. It would have enough gravity to cause light to return to itself. A person would have to travel faster than the speed of light to escape its pull.

How a Black Hole Forms

Most astronomers believe that a black hole forms from the death of a giant star. When a star that has more than three times the mass of the Sun explodes, it becomes a super-nova. Such a star throws off much of its mass and energy. A great cloud of matter is

What a supernova may look like up close

blown into space. For a short period of time, the star can give off as much energy as an entire galaxy.

Once this energy and matter is gone, gravity causes the core of the star to shrink.

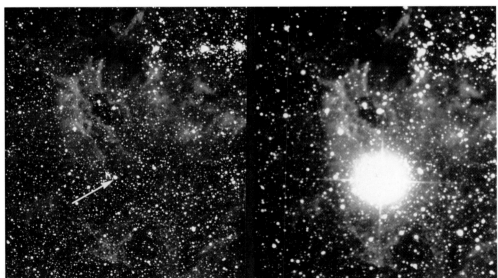

The top photograph shows an expanding gas cloud from a supernova. The bottom photographs show a star before (left) and after (right) it exploded into a supernova.

The crushing weight of matter falling inward from all sides compresses the dying star into a tight, extremely dense mass. When the star shrinks to 60 miles (100 km) in diameter or less, it is called a neutron star.

A false-color image of Cygnus X-2, a possible neutron star

A neutron star is so dense that one teaspoon of its material would weigh 100 million tons on Earth! The gravity of a neutron star is so

The tremendous gravity of a neutron star (at right) pulls matter away from a nearby companion star.

strong that it pulls almost all of its energy back to the star. If a companion star is close enough, matter will be pulled from it into the neutron star.

The only energy that escapes from a neutron star comes from the north and south magnetic poles. When this happens, the star is called a pulsar. If the collapse process continues, the pulsar will eventually become a black hole.

However, black holes may not always come from single stars. Astronomers believe that most large galaxies have a giant black hole at their center. The giant black hole pulls

An artist's impression of what a galactic black hole might look like

In this X-ray image of the center of our galaxy, the bright spots are thought to be X rays—energy in the form of radiation—being released by a massive black hole.

in more and more stars. As it does, it becomes more massive, and its gravity becomes more powerful. Astronomers think there is a giant black hole "eating out" the center of our own Milky Way galaxy.

How Would a Black Hole Look?

Scientists have never seen a black hole. But they do have a good idea of what one looks like. Imagine a black ball in space. It is not very large. Inside it you would see nothing. The surface of this ball would be called the

This diagram of a black hole shows what happens to light coming near it. The five white lines are light rays. The light ray that comes closest to the black hole gets drawn in by the black hole's intense gravity. The "edge" of the ball is the event horizon. The tiny black dot in the center is the singularity.

event horizon. This is the place from which light can no longer escape.

Deep inside the black hole we would come to its center. This is called the singularity. Here all things disappear from our universe as we know them.

The distance between the event horizon and singularity is called the Schwartzchild radius. This measures the actual size of a black hole.

Where Are Black Holes Found?

It is impossible to see a black hole, since one would be looking for a tiny black ball against the blackness of space. Instead, astronomers use clues to find black holes without actually seeing them. They observe how a black hole may affect a nearby star or gas cloud.

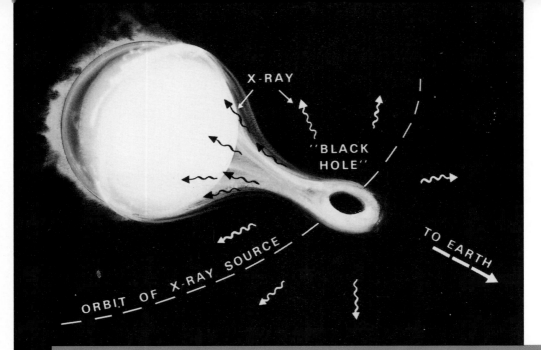

This is a diagram of the black hole discovered in the constellation Cygnus the Swan. As the black hole pulled matter from a nearby star (the white ball), it released energy in the form of X rays. These X rays were what told scientists that a black hole was there. The black hole itself was invisible.

The first possible discovery of a black hole was made by a satellite searching for X rays—extremely tiny high-energy particles—in space. The satellite was looking in the constellation of Cygnus the Swan when it found X rays that seemed to be coming from a star. This was puzzling, because most stars are not hot enough to emit large amounts of X rays.

Black holes, however, do emit X rays. As matter from a nearby star falls into a black hole, it is converted into energy in the form of high temperatures. This energy is released from the black hole as X rays. On closer study, the X rays

The Accretion Disk

Although black holes appear black, most are believed to be surrounded by a bright disk of energy. A black hole pulls in material, rips it apart, and releases huge amounts of energy. As long as a black hole consumes matter, it will have this bright disk around it.

found by the satellite were shown to have been coming from a point very close to the star. This made a strong case for a black hole.

Since the 1970s, astronomers have found several possible black holes. Perhaps the best example lies in the heart of the galaxy called M87. A huge blast of matter and energy has been observed coming from its center. This may be because there are so many stars crowded there. A giant black hole

The core of galaxy M87

could be pulling in what it left behind after blowing the stars apart. Such a giant black hole could be more than 3 billion times the mass of the Sun. It could be the most powerful object in the universe!

Strange Things Would Happen

If you got close to a black hole, strange things would happen. As you got near one, it would slowly pull you, just as if you were approaching any other large body in space. After a while, you would feel yourself moving faster and

An X-ray image of galaxy M87 that suggests that a black hole may lie at its core

faster. By the time you would be moving as fast as light, you would be at the event horizon of the black hole. That is, if you could survive the trip.

If you were falling head first into a black hole, you would look very strange. Your head would get stretched out and become much farther from your feet. You would get taller, but would become very skinny. Why? Since the force of gravity between two objects increases as they come closer together, gravity would be pulling on your head more strongly than on your feet.

A Final Frontier

An astronomer can peer through a telescope and see across both space and time. It takes so long for the light from a distant galaxy to reach us that we see the galaxy as it was long ago, not as it is today.

The study of black holes includes both astronomy and physics. Scientists use astronomy

This photograph of Deep Space shows a cluster of distant galaxies. It takes so long for the light from these galaxies to reach us that we see the galaxies not as they look now, but as they looked long ago.

to help discover black holes, and physics to understand them. But there are many unanswered questions about black holes. Since it is impossible to see what happens inside of black holes, they are still very much a mystery.

To Find Out More

Here are some additional resources to help you learn more about black holes:

 Books

Asimov, Isaac. **Mysteries of Deep Space: Blackholes, Pulsars, and Quasars.** Gareth Stevens, 1994.

Asimov, Isaac. **How Did We Find Out About Black Holes?** Walker & Company, 1978.

Berger, Melvin. **Quasars, Pulsars, and Black Holes in Space.** Putnams' Sons, 1977.

Preston, Richard. **First Light: The Search for the Edge of the Universe.** Penguin, 1987.

Sipiera, Paul P. **Galaxies.** Children's Press, 1997.

Sipiera, Paul P. **Stars.** Children's Press, 1997.

Organizations

**Astronomical Society of
the Pacific**
1290 24th Avenue
San Francisco, CA 94122
*http://www.physics.sfsu.ed
u/asp*

**Junior Astronomical
Society**
58 Vaughan Gardens
Ilford Essex IG1 3PD
England

The Planetary Society
5 North Catalina Avenue
Pasadena, CA 91106
email: *tps.lc@genie.geis.
com*

Online Sites

Astronet
*http://www.xs4all.nl/~
carlkop/astroeng.html*

**Exploring Our Solar
System—and Beyond**
*http://www.reston.com/
astro/explore.html*

**The Planetary Studies
Foundation**
*http://homepage.
interaccess.com/~jpatpsf/>.*

Important Words

astronomer scientist who studies the stars, planets, and other heavenly bodies

event horizon the surface of a black hole

galaxy billions of stars revolving around a common center of gravity

neutron particle found in the nucleus of most atoms; it has no electrical charge

neutron star star made almost entirely of closely packed neutrons; it can form after a supernova explosion causes a massive star to collapse

Schwartzchild radius the distance between singularity and the event horizon of a black hole

singularity the center of mass of a black hole, where gravity is so strong that the mass has been crushed to a ball with no diameter at all

supernova explosion at the end of a massive star's lifetime that leaves a debris cloud and a dense core that may become a neutron star

Index

Meet the Author

Paul P. Sipiera is a professor of geology and astronomy at William Rainey Harper College in Palatine, Illinois. His main area of research is meteorites. When he is not studying science, he can be found working on his farm in Galena, Illinois, with his wife, Diane, and their two daughters Andrea and Paula Frances.